IMAGES
of England

MIDDLETON

Thatched cottages, Idlers' Corner, Long Street (opposite King Street). The stone flag walls, peculiar to this part of Lancashire, were useful to rest against half way up a hill, hence the name given to this spot.

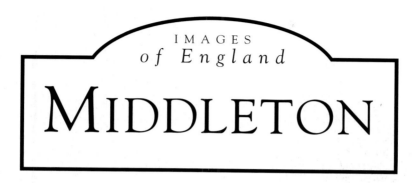

IMAGES
of England

MIDDLETON

Compiled by
Hannah Haynes and Carl Goldberg

TEMPUS

Acknowledgements

With grateful thanks to Geoffrey Wellens for the loan of photographs and for help and encouragement. Photographs from the collections of the late Frank Cosgrove and Stanley White are gratefully acknowledged. Thanks also to Lawrance Kaye, Jim Mckeown, Middleton Civic Association, Middleton Guardian, St. Leonard's Church and other friends for permission to use their photographs. The help given to us by Pat Elliott and Jean Francis of Middleton Local Studies Library was also very much appreciated.

Dedication

In memory of our friend and local historian, Stanley White.

First published 1995, reprinted 2003

Tempus Publishing Limited
The Mill, Brimscombe Port,
Stroud, Gloucestershire, GL5 2QG

© Hannah Haynes and Carl Goldberg, 1995

The right of Hannah Haynes and Carl Goldberg to be identified as the Authors of this work has been asserted in accordance with the Copyrights, Designs and Patents Act 1988.

British Library Cataloguing in Publication Data.
A catalogue record for this book is available from the British Library.

ISBN 0 7524 0344 3

Typesetting and origination by Tempus Publishing Limited
Printed in Great Britain by Midway Colour Print, Wiltshire

Contents

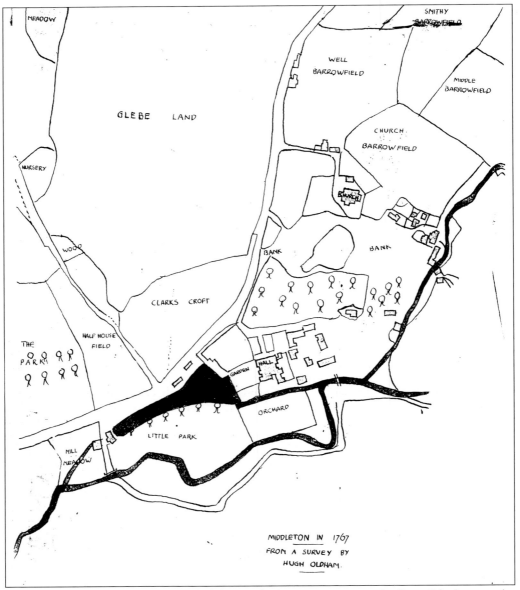

Hugh Oldham's Map of 1767. The dark line at the bottom represents the River Irk, forming the boundary between Middleton Township and the Townships of Tonge and Alkrington.

Introduction

A book of 200 photographs provides an excellent means of illustrating the way in which Middleton developed from a village surrounded by scattered halls, folds and farms into a thriving mill town and then into Middleton as we know it today. It also presents the challenge of capturing something of Middleton's renowned individual character. Middleton has seen many boundary changes and today includes Alkrington, Birch, Langley, Mills Hill, Rhodes, Tonge and parts of Hopwood and Thornham.

The name Middleton is thought to be of Saxon origin, as is that of Thornham and the two always appear to have been linked. The de Middleton family were landowners in the 12th century, the first recorded reference to them being in 1183 when Roger de Middleton made a grant of land in Ashworth. He also granted land to the monks of Stanlaw Abbey. The Manor of Middleton was annexed to the Honour of Clitheroe, held by the de Lacy family and later by the Earls and Dukes of Lancaster. Settlements at Stanycliffe, Langley and Hopwood were also ancient, dating back to at least the 12th and 13th centuries.

The de Middletons were followed by the de Bartons and the Asshetons as Lords of the Manor of Middleton, whose vast Middleton and Thornham Estates were largely occupied by tenant farmers. The first Sir Ralph Assheton was appointed Vice Constable of England for outstanding bravery in the War of the Roses and his grandson, Richard, was knighted on Flodden Field in 1513 for his heroism in leading the Middleton Archers in battle. Ralph Assheton, born in 1605, was largely responsible for the defeat of the Royalist forces at Manchester in 1642. Although the Assheton family achieved national recognition during the time they held the Manor (1438-1765), Middleton remained very much a village. The widow of the last Sir Ralph was opposed to growth and made every effort to keep the village "uncontaminated by vulgar workshops".

It was not until Harbord Harbord (who later became Lord Suffield) became Lord of the Manor by marriage in 1765, that land was leased for development. The first leases were in 1776 alongside the turnpike which is now Long Street. As silk weaving was introduced into Middleton in 1778, many of the new tenants were weavers working on hand-looms in their cottages. Some of them still worked the plough and hoe as well as the new shuttles and winding wheels. Middleton's "stamp of its own", was noted by Mr Angus Reach, a London reporter for the *Morning Chronicle*, who visited Middleton in 1849. He commented, "some of the oldest and purest blood of the Lancashire yeomen kept its current unmixed by the hearths of the village". The weavers still followed the rural and patriarchal way of bygone times and were described as clannish and of an "individual tone of character." However, many had an extraordinary zest for education and an enterprising spirit, much of their education coming from the Sunday Schools and night schools.

Some weavers formed clubs, which were an early form of co-operative society or building society, to finance the building of their cottages. These club houses were in the Church Street, King Street, Union Street area above St. Leonard's Church, known as Top O' Middleton. When Angus Reach asked to see a club house he found a dozen cocks and hens scratching the earth floor beneath four looms! The living room however was stone-flagged, sanded and clean, with excellent cooking ranges on either side of the grate, a typical feature of the Middleton weavers' cottages. Some weavers moved into co-operative textile design and production, manufacturing velvet jackets. They took over a farm at Jumbo, which they nicknamed Lowbands, for their textile venture and also for co-operative farming. The origins of the C.W.S. can be traced back to early enterprises such as these.

Lord Suffield (Harbord Harbord) obtained a Market Charter in 1791. The success of the early hand-loom weavers brought silk mills to the town and the manufacture of silk ribbons, used for hat bands, medals and braidings, continued until the middle of this century. From around 1800 cotton spinning mills were built and all branches of cotton manufacture were to be found in the town by 1833. Abundance of a pure water supply, improved methods of transport and a strategic position in the heart of Lancashire's cotton belt also brought many bleachers and dyers to Middleton. Among them was Salis Schwabe, who ceased to practise Judaism after he came to Middleton in 1832. The Schwabe family's influence in Rhodes was considerable, providing employment, housing, library, reading room, schools and other facilities. The "Chimney School" was established in 1837 and replaced by the new school building in 1884. Boardman Lane is featured as an example of a Rhodes' street whose land was leased from Sir Harbord Harbord and whose occupants benefitted from the Schwabe family's enterprises.

Middleton's dramatic transformation from village to industrial town was not without its tragedies. On the 20th April 1812, Luddites attacked the power-loom weaving mill of Messrs. Daniel Burton and Sons at Wood Street and four of them were killed (the Luddites opposed the use of new machinery). Samuel Bamford fought for reform on behalf of Lancashire's labouring classes and led a contingent from Middleton to Manchester, where several people were massacred at Peterloo in 1819.

Calico printing, jam making, rubber making, iron founding and other trades brought employment for Middleton's increasing population. Middleton was incorporated as a borough in 1886, at which time the population figure was 20,000. It became part of the Metropolitan Borough of Rochdale in 1974. Tonge was formerly in the parish of Prestwich-cum-Oldham and it was not until the Improvement Act of 1861 that it became united with Middleton. Alkrington and parts of Hopwood came under Middleton between 1879 and 1886.

Standing guard over the town, throughout all the changes, is the Parish Church of St. Leonard. The first reference to the Norman church appears in 1183, but a church, with maybe a castle close by, is thought to have stood on its site from Saxon times. The tower arch, which appears to be early Norman, is the only remaining 12th century feature, the church having been largely rebuilt by Thomas Langley in 1412 and again by Sir Ralph Assheton in 1524, the latter as a thank offering for the victory of Flodden Field. The detached portions of the parish of St. Leonard were as far afield as Great Lever, Ainsworth and Ashworth. Before chapels-of-ease were established, families were faced with a long journey, often on foot, to St. Leonard's for weddings and other services and many employed a fiddler to keep up their spirits on the way. The sight of the church on the hill coming into view would no doubt have been very welcome!

The famous "Nowster" curfew bell was rung every night between 9.50 and 10 p.m. from the time of the Luddite attacks in 1812, to the beginning of World War II, when church bells were silenced. The use of a curfew bell dates back nationally to Norman times, when it was the signal for fires and lights to be extinguished. In more recent years the Nowster Bell has been rung to mark special occasions.

One

Rural Beginnings

The Lords of the Manor lived at Middleton Hall. Hopwood Hall had its own large estate with farms, cottages and a corn mill and it remained in the Hopwood and Gregge-Hopwood families until 1940. Many other smaller halls and their farms, with folds or hamlets close by, were scattered around Middleton. Hopwood, Tonge and Alkrington Halls have survived, the former two dating back largely to Tudor times and the latter to Georgian. Halls such as Stakehill were lost when land was taken for development. Many of Middleton's former green fields are now occupied by housing developments, such as those at Alkrington and Langley but a number of farms have survived. The villages of Birch and Bowlee retained much of their old world character well into this century and Thornham Fold and Tandle Hill remain unspoilt, with land around them still being farmed. Some former agricultural buildings such as the White Houses at Rhodes found themselves adapting to the industrial revolution by housing coachmen and carters for the nearby Rhodes' Works.

"Harvest Home". Tenant farmers were obliged to bring their grain to be ground at the Lord of the Manor's mill near Middleton Hall. The Hall stood between the old Market Place and Oldham Road, looking south towards the Irk, on what is now Old Hall Street.

Part of the Middleton Hall premises in 1791. The half-timbered Hall was largely rebuilt in 1805 but was demolished in 1845. Both illustrations on this page are taken from an old jug which is housed at Middleton Library.

The Tithe Barn, formerly in the Rectory grounds on the site of Mellalieu Street.

Old cottages, including a smithy, on Long Street. The large sign reads "Site for New Wesleyan Church". Long Street Methodist Church (see the photograph at the bottom of page 84) was opened on the site in 1902.

The Old Boar's Head Inn on the old great highway to Yorkshire (now Long Street). It was featured in the works of Edwin Waugh, Rochdale poet and miscellaneous writer.

The Old Boar's Head c.1875. Its half-timbered style is typical of early Lancashire domestic buildings and it appears to have been part of a row of cottages before it became an inn. A stone lintel in the cellar is dated 1632. A licensee was recorded as early as 1737.

Stanycliffe Hall c.1890. It was a half-timbered building dating back to the early 16th century, standing on a cliff above Hopwood and Blomeley Cloughs. Stanycliffe Bridge below was described in 1831 as in a "dangerous and precipitous hollow ", where many serious coach accidents occurred. Twelfth century records mention an earlier hall which Baron Montbegon, a Norman overlord, granted to the Knights Hospitallers of St. John of Jerusalem, who had a chapel there.

The Warren and Gypsy Croft, looking towards the Old Boar's Head. In 1889 Jubilee Park and Middleton Library were opened in the former Croft.

Hopwood Hall c.1890. William de Hopwood lived at a hall on the site in 1277. This present building largely dates back to the time of Henry VIII, when it was surrounded by a moat. It is a rare example of the early use of bricks in Lancashire.

The Corn Mill on the lower pond of the Hopwood Hall Estate. It was demolished about 1946, when the Estate was taken over by De La Salle College, but its remains can still be seen.

Langley Hall, demolished in 1885. Geoffrey de Langley, who fought alongside Richard I in the 12th century, is thought to have lived at an earlier hall on the site. Thomas Langley, Lord Chancellor of England and Cardinal Prince Bishop of Durham was born here about 1360.

Tonge Hall, dating back to about 1590. It remained in the Tonge family until the end of the last century, when William Assheton Tonge offered it as a gift to the town for use as a museum. Sadly, his offer was refused but the Wolstencroft family have since restored the Hall for use as their family home.

Alkrington Hall with its former 700 acre estate overlooking the River Irk. This Georgian building replaced an earlier hall and was built from bricks baked on the site. For generations it was the home of the Lever Family and at one time housed Sir Ashton Lever's Museum.

High Barn Farm, Alkrington, built about 1700 and demolished July 1968.

Wood Cottage in Alkrington Woods, taken from Nut Bank, 9 July 1939. The cottage dates back to 1733, when D'Arcy Lever owned Alkrington Hall. In 1939 the cottage still had its own well and was surrounded by wooden palings to keep out the rabbits. Seventy acres of Alkrington Wood became Corporation property in 1936.

Brown's Farm and cottages (off Hilton Fold Lane) with Little Green mine shaft. The latter is a reminder of the importance of coal mining in Middleton, the seam being the Royley seam. The manager's son is reputed to have hung himself from the pit head gear, thus resulting in the farm being known as Gallows Pit Farm.

Boardman Fold Farm, Moss Lane, taken from the west, 23 February 1937.

Lancashire Fold, Sunk Lane 1936. It was situated at the junction of what is now Kirkway and Mount Road and the toll bar against the post of the iron gate is on the drive to "The Mount."

Lancashire Fold Farm, demolished along with the Fold when the Alkrington Housing Estate was built.

Stakehill Hall Farm, demolished for the Stakehill Industrial Estate. A settlement at Stakehill dates back to at least 1330.

Thornham Fold in the 1980s. Thorn and Ham are both words of Saxon origin. The course of Thornham Lane has altered slightly over the years and it passed in front of these cottages at one time. Packhorses are thought to have been stabled in the Fold.

Hebers Hall Farm. It was built about 1882 when John Shepherd became tenant farmer of its 29 acres. He had farmed in the area prior to it being built.

Hebers Hall Farm milk float with Miss Ann Shepherd as driver in Jubilee Road c.1898. In the early days everyone had to collect their milk from the farms.

Peel Terrace, Heywood Road, Birch, with the Old Three Tuns Inn to the left. Whittle Lane is on the left around the corner.

A closeup of the Old Three Tuns Inn, 451 Heywood Road, 1890. The Inn was closed in 1913 and demolished about 1923, by which time most of the surrounding property had already gone.

Simon Lane Farm on Bowlee Common. Joss and Jim Bentley farmed here before World War I, followed by the Hydes and the Hardys, the latter moving to Simon Lane from nearby Egypt Farm.

Sheep and cattle being driven along Long Street c.1900.

23

Bowlee Road (now Heywood Old Road) with Little Nook to the right.

A close up of Little Nook Cottages and Farm, Rhodes.

Rhodes Green Farm milk float belonging to the Coates family. The driver, Roy Hilton, has Frank Cosgrove with him.

Haymaking at Rhodes Green Farm c.1928. Left to right are Walter Coates, Kenneth Metcalfe, Frank Cosgrove (at the front with the black tie), Arthur Tippet (back) and George Metcalfe.

An "important member of the family" at Rhodes Green Farm 1927, with Walter Coates and Lillian.

The White Houses in Manchester Old Road c.1922. They were demolished in 1936 for road widening. They used to have a farmyard and dairy behind them. Later coachmen and carters for the Schwabe family and then Calico Printers Association lived in the cottages. Large horse drawn carts collected coal from Middleton Station and also took finished calico prints to Manchester warehouses. The sign reads, "This way to the Cricket Ground".

Two

Times of Change

The hand-loom weavers and the silk mills that sprang up around them continued long after the industrial revolution brought cotton spinning mills to Middleton. The last silk weavers were still at their looms towards the end of the 19th century as power machines could not match their skill with fine yarns like silk. But cotton was certainly "king" by 1833 and Middleton's population was rapidly increasing as people desperate for employment moved in from the country. Many former weavers' cottages survived until the middle of this century, but few remain today. With the factory age came blocks of terraced houses such as the Lark Hill development of the 1860s. The neat rows of houses had communal yards behind them, originally containing middens used for ashes and nightsoil. All were swept away in the Compulsory Purchase Orders of the 1960s, making way for developments with less density of housing. The abundance of water, which attracted the bleachers and dyers to the town, was not always a blessing, as the vivid pictures of the floods illustrate!

Joseph Briggs, aged 84, still loyal to his hand-loom (silk) at 40 Wood Street in the 1890s. He was one of Middleton's last hand-loom weavers. The caption should read hand-loom weaving not winding.

Former weavers' cottages at Spring Gardens. These early cottages, built on land leased from Lord Suffield in the 1780s and '90s, were tiny and in sharp contrast to loomhouses built later.

28

Hannah Street former weavers' cottages. The upper windows are of a type popular in Middleton and known as Yorkshire lights. The glass panes measured 5 inches by 9 inches and they were set in frames, the centre one of which could be moved behind the outer ones. The houses were demolished in the 1960s.

Loomhouses at the corner of Irk Street and Simpson Street.

The former Hebers' Workhouse or Poor House. Middleton, Hopwood, Pilsworth, Thornham and Birtle-cum-Bamford townships all contributed to its upkeep. It is a reminder of the days prior to the formation of the Oldham Poor Law Union of which Middleton became a part. The cottages were demolished in 1936.

St. Leonard's Square c.1900. Number 21 New Lane, which is to the left of Church Street, was demolished in 1964. The house to its left, demolished in 1946, was of a cruck frame construction dating back to at least the early 16th century.

Delivering milk among the former club houses on King Street, a reminder of times when the pace of life was more leisurely. These houses and many others in the surrounding streets above St. Leonard's were financed by building clubs, a form of early co-operative, whose members were mainly hand-loom silk weavers. As a result, more houses were owned by their occupiers in Middleton in the early 1800s, than in any similar sized town in England.

Number 61 Union Street. The plaque read "Samuel Bamford, reformer resided and was arrested in this house Aug 26 1819". Bamford led the ill-fated Middleton contingent to Peterloo. He was also a poet and a hand-loom silk weaver. Union Street was comprised of club houses, hence its name. It was demolished in 1963.

Tandle Hill War Memorial, 1956 (before it was vandalised). It was unveiled by Lord Derby in October 1921. Tandle Hill was mentioned during evidence concerning the Peterloo Massacre in 1819, when a weaver from Stakehill testified that over 500 men had been drilled there. Trees were planted to discourage Chartists and other groups from gathering. The land passed from the Suffields to Joseph Milne and then to Norris Bradbury, who gave Tandle Hill as a peace thanksgiving for use as a public park. This was opened two years prior to the Memorial being unveiled and Tandle Hill now has country park status.

Wash Day at Jumbo in the 1890s. Mrs Heaton is on the left, at the top right is Mrs Jagger with the Johnson sisters second from the right on both rows. Interestingly, the women look just as proud as those in the picture below!

Suffragettes attracting the curiosity of male passers-by in Market Place. Nationally famous figures such as Ada Pankhurst, daughter of Emmeline, came to Middleton between 1904 and 1914. The photograph was taken by Walter Moore (see also the photograph at the top of page 92).

Aerial View of Lark Hill, 1939, with St. Peter's Church (on Taylor Street) to the left and St. Michael, Tonge behind. The streets from the bottom upwards are: Hannah Street, Oldham Road, Albert Street, Victoria Street, Gladstone Street, Ogden Street, Tetlow Street and Peach Bank. Wince Brook is behind and Ashton Lane to the right. Neva Mills (formerly Dane) are at the top left with a small section of the railway leading from Middleton Station to Middleton Junction. The two churches remain but virtually everything else was swept away in the Compulsory Purchase Orders of the 1960s.

Number 2, Albert Street. Tin bath, dolly tubs, mangle, clothes props, washing line, step ladders, shovel and even a toilet seat are neatly stored at the back of the house in the communal yard.

Barges on the Rochdale Canal at Slattocks Bridge. The Canal was opened in 1804 and was used mainly to transport stone, coal and lime.

The horse drawn 'bus was one of the early forms of public transport and conductor Charles Campbell is ready to collect the fares. Licensee Harriet Lees is next to driver John Fitton outside the Old Roebuck Inn c.1900.

Hilton Fold Tram Shed. The horse is Merriman who was used to pull overhead repair wagons and for other duties. Mr Davies is holding Merriman with Mr Everall behind him.

Tram-track re-laying in Oldham Road, with Vincent Pearson just to the right of centre.

Tram at Middleton Junction by J. W. Lees' Brewery, with the conductor posing for the camera.

Daimler motor bus with solid tyres, 1919. This form of transport had only just been introduced and people used to complain about the noise it made on the stone setts. Sometimes gas mantles were damaged by the vibration!

Damage caused by a gas explosion at West End Co-op, 1909. The building was on the corner of Boothroyden Road and Manchester Old Road, Rhodes.

Gas Works Brow bridge where Joseph Stansfield was drowned on 11 July 1927. The River Irk had burst its banks causing the canal embankment at Mills Hill to collapse. Boats from Heaton Park Lake were called into action to aid rescue after this catastrophic flood.

Clearing up at Little Park after the 1927 flood. Ralph is searching for his half-crown at the bottom right of the photograph! The Jolly Butcher Inn and the Warwick and Irk Mills can be seen behind.

Cleaning up in Irk Street after the 1927 flood. The centre of Middleton is at the confluence of the Irk and the Wince and Whit Brooks and consequently is liable to flooding.

More recent flooding in 1967, showing a partly submerged van behind the Post Office.

Three
Streets of Middleton

A Roman Road from Chester to York is thought to have passed through Middleton. Manchester Old Road and Long Street were certainly part of the great highway from Manchester to York and they were turnpiked in 1754, following the Manchester and Rochdale Turnpike Act. The route from Manchester was via Crumpsall with a toll house at Rhodes. In 1804 an alternative route was opened via Blackley. The early route became Manchester Old Road and the other Manchester New Road. Heywood Road (now Heywood Old Road) was also turnpiked. Thornham Lane is a very ancient track and was presumably part of the road from Middleton to Milnrow mentioned in Rochdale's Manor Survey of 1626. Many of Middleton's old lanes were on private estates and some of their toll bars remained until the late 1940s. In 1895, the Corporation successfully appealed to the agent for Hopwood Hall for a reduction in charges at the Hebers' Toll Bar. The new rate was 1d for each horse, 2d for horse and 2 wheeled vehicle, 3d for horse and 4 wheeled vehicle, 1s for a traction engine and 3d for a dozen sheep or oxen. Boardman Lane is featured in this section as typical of the new streets built on land leased from Sir Harbord Harbord in the 1780s.

Birch Toll Bar, Heywood Road (now Heywood Old Road) in the 1860s. It faced the White Hart Inn, opposite the bottom of Langley Lane. Policeman Wise stands in the centre with Samuel Kay, landlord of the Black Bull Inn, to the left and Tom Elliott, clogger, in the middle of the gateway. The boy leaning against the tollhouse is Tom Jacques who later became schoolmaster of Birch. Being a very early photograph, the women's manner of dress is of special interest. The Toll House was demolished when Langley Lane was widened. Toll houses and bars were familiar sights on turnpike roads and old private lanes and in addition to those illustrated there were bars at Rhodes, Tonge Lane, Mills Hill and Alkrington Green.

Hebers' Toll House 1909, with Hebers' Workhouse behind. The Toll House was on Hollin Lane and remained until 1949. "Owd" Richard Cowburn, butler at Hopwood Hall, lived there at one time, followed by Jim Cowburn and his wife.

Thornham Lane Toll House. The board displaying the list of charges is above the large window. In the 1930s it read "To be demanded at the Stakehill and Hathershaw Moor Bar. Toll of $1\frac{1}{2}$d per wheel is now charged..." Charges were waived during the War and discontinued in 1946.

Boardman Lane and residents in the early 1920s. The chimneys of Rhodes Weaving Shed (left) and Highouses Limited can be seen on Factory Brow behind. "Da" Wilding is standing on the left with Alice Cosgrove (in the doorway) to her left. Betty Wilding can be seen on the right with Ethel Kent, Gladys Reid, Elsie Reid, Ada Pilling and Florence Craddock between them. Land for the houses numbered 92-96 (front left) was leased from Sir Harbord Harbord in 1786. The lease stipulated that houses built thereon should have walls 15 inches thick, the bricks be bought from Middleton Brick Company (owned by Harbord Harbord) and any grain grown on land at the rear had to be milled at Middleton Mill, which was also owned by him. Like so many of Middleton's old streets that were full of life and character, Boardman Lane was swept away in the Compulsory Purchase Orders of the 1950s and '60s, numbers 92-96 being demolished in 1964.

Auntie Nellie Stott's sweet shop, 92 Boardman Lane.

"In the Gutter", 1929. Many people took great pride in the appearance of their streets. Alice Cosgrove is caught by the camera whilst cleaning the flags outside her house at 94 Boardman Lane.

Alice Cosgrove wearing her Sunday best in 1934, in the Chapel Street Primitive Methodist Sunday School procession in Boardman Lane. Ida Wilding is to her right with Elsie, Gladys and Bessie Reid behind. Their clothes contrast sharply with the clogs and shawls of the girls behind on the right.

The George VI Coronation street party, Boardman Lane, 1937.

"The corner shop", now becoming a thing of the past. This one was at the bottom of Chapel Street, Rhodes, on its corner with Walker Street.

Heywood Old Road and Langley Lane junction, Birch, after the Toll House had been demolished. The bay-windowed row was built in the 1890s. All the houses were demolished in the C.P.O.s of the 1950s and '60s (compare with the photograph on page 42).

Heywood Old Road just to the south of the previous photograph. These houses had been built for workers at nearby Birch Mill.

Bowlee Brow (Heywood Old Road) with Bowlee Co-op on the left.

Looking down Bowlee Brow, 1949, with Bowlee Methodist Church (built 1864) to the right.

Grimshaw Lane near Lancashire Fold.

Mills Hill Road, Middleton Junction.

Manchester Old Road with Rhodes Chimney dominating the village. The Gardeners Arms is on the left.

Manchester Old Road with the town centre mill chimneys coming into view.

The junction of Manchester Old and New Roads, with the Edgar Wood Fountain to the left of centre.

Central Gardens looking rather stark just after their opening in October 1934. They soon became colourful and were a valued asset at the junction of Manchester Old and New Roads. The Edgar Wood Fountain had been moved to Oldham Road, where it remained until it was demolished in 1960.

Central Gardens taken from the Manchester Old Road side, 28 June 1973.

Back o'th' Brow, showing the prominent position of St. Leonard's on the skyline. The Old Grammar School is to the left of centre.

Church Street looking towards St. Leonard's Square, 3 May 1946.

Market Day at the old Market Place c.1930. The market dated back to 1791, when Lord Suffield was granted a Charter to hold weekly markets on Fridays.

Market Place, then at the heart of Middleton.

Market Place taken from a more unusual angle.

Market Place Gardens. These attractive ornamental gardens were laid out on the old Market Ground in 1948/9, after the market had moved to Fountain Street.

Long Street with St. Leonard's steeple above.

Looking the opposite way down Long Street in 1959/60. The Post Office is on the right, on the corner of Sadler Street, the building at the left of the block is the Co-op Central Stores.

Long Street in the early 1900s with the Parish Church School and Middleton Library to the right. The library was opened on 9 March 1889 as Jubilee Free Library, the plans originating in Queen Victoria's Diamond Jubilee year. Jubilee Park was opened in July 1889.

Long Street between the Hare and Hounds Inn and Cheapside c.1910 (see also the photograph at the top of page 96).

Suffield Square Gardens in Middleton Centre, 1992.

Aerial View of Middleton, 1937.

Four

Wooden Steeple

A wooden steeple at St. Leonard's dates back to at least the seventeenth century. The rhyme goes "Wooden steeple, stubborn people" and Canon Durnford described them as "too apt to disbelieve what they ought to believe, and to believe what they ought to disbelieve". St. Leonard's has served its people from at least 1183, being largely rebuilt in 1412 and 1524. It was not able to accommodate all the worshippers from Middleton's rapidly increasing population during the industrial revolution. The Government stepped in with money from its "Million Pounds Church Fund", voted by Parliament as a thank offering for victory at Waterloo. No doubt there was some spiritual aim in providing money to build churches in areas experiencing sudden growth but the motivation was also "lest a Godless people become a rebellious people". St. Mary, Birch was a Waterloo Church, as was St. Michael, Tonge. Middleton also has a strong Non-Conformist tradition typical of many Lancashire towns. Before the advent of the Welfare State the churches provided a cradle to grave service. "Waifs and Strays" and "Sick and Burial" societies abounded and a "death class" was common. Spiritual welfare and grim realities were catered for but so was the social side of life, with bands, cricket teams, bazaars and a host of other activities.

St. Leonard's Parish Church Middleton, 1 June 1902. The flag flies because the photograph was taken on the day victory was declared in the Boer War.

The Middleton Archers depicted with their names in the Flodden Window of St. Leonard's Church. The window is the oldest glazed war memorial in England.

The interior of St. Leonard's looking west, before major restoration work.

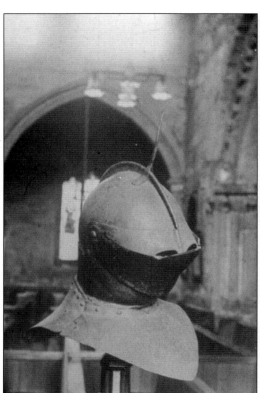

Sir Richard Assheton presented his armour to St. Leonard's after the Battle of Flodden. Tradition has it that this is his helmet.

John Stock Feoffees' Loaves. Twelve sixpenny loaves were laid out for the poor in St. Leonard's every Sunday, as a result of John Stock's Charity. The feoffees (trustees) also paid for two boy and two girl apprentices each year.

Middleton Parish Church hand-bell ringers in 1853. Left to right are, Thomas Arrowsmith, Thomas Fallows, Thomas Buckley, James Buckley, Samuel Saxon and John Heywood.

St. Leonard's bell ringers of 1937. Tom Driver is front left with John Hollows, sixty years a bell ringer, to his right. John Smith is at the back right with Abraham Ogden to his left.

The Old Rectory of St. Leonard's. It used to be surrounded by a moat with drawbridge and wooden bridge-house and some walls had loopholes through which arrows could be fired. It underwent considerable restoration in the 1870s, when it lost its half-timbered appearance and it is now privately owned.

Sherwood and Stanton Jones, two brothers who both became bishops. Both were Rectors of St. Leonard's, Stanton from 1912-1920, with Sherwood taking over from him and continuing until 1945.

Rector Sherwood Jones passing the New Inn, Long Street in the St. Leonard's procession.

The girls of St. Leonard's Sunday School at the bottom of Barrowfields. West and North Streets are to the right. Most churches processed into surrounding streets at Whitsuntide, when scholars proudly displayed their new clothes. Some also "walked" on Sunday School anniversaries.

The Church of St. Mary, Birch, built in 1827, with its National School to the left (see also the photograph at the top of page 112).

Spilling out into the parish on the St. Mary, Birch Anniversary of 1 July 1911.

The beautiful interior of St. Mary, Birch. For many years St. Mary's congregation thrived but as the nearby mills declined they found themselves very much "out in the fields". The Waterloo church was demolished in 1964 and replaced by a smaller building.

The Waterloo Church of St. Michael, Tonge, consecrated 5 October 1839. It was later extended and rebuilt.

Holy Trinity, Parkfield, Waifs and Strays Society with Vicar, Reverend Thomas Townsend c.1930.

An early Holy Trinity procession. Holy Trinity, Parkfield is a daughter church of St. Leonard's. It was built in 1862, when Canon Richard Durnford was Rector of St. Leonard's and he was largely responsible for its establishment in the recently developed area of Parkfield. The land had previously been part of the Great Park attached to Middleton Hall. The first incumbent, Rev. Emery Bates, moved to Holy Trinity from St. Leonard's. Holy Trinity's stained glass windows are noteworthy, especially the west window.

Holy Trinity Cricket Team.

Temple Street Baptist Church Bazaar, held 8-13 July 1914. The tent is in the field at the side of the church.

St. Peter's R.C. Church Whit Walk at the junction of Victoria Street and Gilmour Street, Lark Hill c.1907. The May Queen is Ada Moran and teacher Annie Moran wears the hat with the flowers. Mr Johnny Boyle, an enthusiastic worker at the church, is on the left.

All Saints, Rhodes, Church Band c.1931.

The attractive All Saints, Rhodes banner.

All Saints, Rhodes, Sunday School procession.

The interior of Rhodes' Wesleyan Methodist Chapel.

Hebers' United Methodist procession.

Harvest Festival at St. Margaret, Boarshaw, c.1956.

Providence Independent Chapel (left) and School, Market Place. It became a Congregational and then United Reformed Chapel. The Providence buildings were closed in 1991 when the congregation was amalgamated with Alkrington U.R.C. Only the church building remains.

Five

Serving the People

The Wellens family are featured as a family that came to Middleton from Wilmslow in the early 18th century and became involved in many aspects of its life. Joseph Wellens was licensee of the Church Fowt in St. Leonard's Square and Ann Wellens later took over the King's Arms. Abraham Wellens, born in the club houses at Wells Buildings, King Street in 1833, became a hand-loom weaver and draper. In 1870 he established an undertaking business, and later, with sons Samuel, a tailor, and Joseph, a joiner, moved to 54 Long Street. Sam's son Billy came into the business in the 1920s. During his Mayoral year he had the honour of laying the foundation stone for the firm's new premises at 121 Long Street. The firm of S. Wellens & Sons have now reached their 125th anniversary and Billy's sons Norman and Geoffrey are celebrating the event in 1995. In fact, the family connection goes back further, as the Oldham Poor Law Union accounts of 1838 include the following : "Samuel Wellens supplied coffin for James Nutt's wife of Jumbo - 14s". Abraham's brother William had a flock mill in the former Hebers' Workhouse and invented one of the first freewheels for bicycles.

Councillor Billy Wellens, Mayor of Middleton 1954-55, on Mayoral Sunday. Left to right outside St. Leonard's Church are A. Horridge (Deputy Mayor), F. Lord Kay, Billy Wellens and F. Johnson (Town Clerk).

Civic plate presented to the Borough by the Mayor, Councillor Billy Wellens.

Councillor Edith P. Wellens as Mayor, 1962-3. She had been Mayoress during her husband Billy's Mayoral year.

The King's Arms with left to right Anne Wellens (nee Slater), Betsy Wellens (nee Jackson), Robert Wellens and Anne Wellens (nee Saxon).

A Dottridge Brothers' horse drawn hearse of 1909, owned by S. Wellens & Sons and restored by them between 1980 and 1985.

Wellens' first Austin, 1924-5.

Part of the procession of cars for the funeral of Charles O. Hulbert in 1936, undertaken by S. Wellens & Sons.

A Boer War parade in Oldham Road.

Fred Saxon (left), a Middleton man who was awarded the Military Medal.

Tank No. 68 in Market Place, 8 November 1919, with Lieut. J.B.Meek of the Tank Corps and Mayor Ald. W.M.Wiggins on the left. It was presented to Middleton by the War Loans Savings Committee in recognition of £600,000 raised by the town. This No.3 type female tank carried 6 machine guns, (2 each side, 1 front and 1 in reserve), and had served on French battle-fields. It's Daimler engine conquered the steep incline of Barrowfields en route to Brassey Street Recreation Ground, where it was imbedded in concrete and remained for many years.

The Garden of Remembrance, Manchester Old Road, with the cross and tablets bearing the names of 691 Middleton men who lost their lives in the Great War. An extension, with the names of those who lost their lives in World War II, was incorporated in 1951.

The Home Guard proudly marching up Long Street during World War II.

A World War II ambulance outside St. Peter's School.

Parkfield House after it became Middleton's second Town Hall. It was demolished November 1978.

Middleton Fire Brigade, Suffield Street, in the 1920s. The horses had to be rescued in the flood of 1927.

The Edgar Wood Fountain, opposite the Brittania Hotel in the Town Centre. Edgar Wood (1860-1935) was an art nouveau architect and artist who introduced a new style of building into Middleton. His first commission of 1887 was this fountain and shelter commemorating Queen Victoria's Jubilee.

Long Street Methodist Church, designed by Edgar Wood in 1899 and opened in 1902. Elm Street and Durnford Street Schools, also designed by him, followed in 1908.

An Edgar Wood house, 165 Manchester Old Road, built in 1912.

Middleton's first Co-op, opened in 1846/7 in Little Park (opposite the Jolly Butcher). The Co-op went under the name of Middleton and Tonge Industrial Society.

The Co-op Hebers branch (no.7). Shutters were essential for many cottages and shops, providing protection from stones flicked up by passing carriages.

The Co-op Lark Hill branch (no.5).

The Co-op Parkfield branch (no.6), opened 27 June 1872.

The Co-op Jumbo branch (no.2), opened Autumn 1875.

Middleton Co-op's
Central Stores, Long
Street, opened 4
November 1871.

Arthur C. Clegg (left) as a young man learning the trade in the Boot and Shoe department of
the Co-op's Central Stores.

Arthur C. Clegg (right) judging an All England shoe repairing competition in London, 1938/9. Arthur was All England champion in 1937. He was a bespoke boot and shoemaker and repairer with a shop at 300 Oldham Road.

Staff outside the C.W.S. Jam and Pickle Works, Mills Hill c.1914.

C.W.S. vinegar exhibition lorry outside the works at Mills Hill.

Christmas Pudding manufacture at the C.W.S. Preserve Works, Mills Hill.

Henry Key's clock and watchmaker's shop, 246 Oldham Road.

A typical clock dial made by John Lees, Middleton's foremost clock maker, working in Middleton 1770-1804.

Walter Moore, artist and photographer, with some of his work displayed outside his baker's shop at 40 Manchester Old Road. Mrs Moore is standing at the back with Mary, whom the Moores had "taken in from the poor house", in front of her. Walter Moore Junior is on the left and Dorothy Moore (now aged 96) is to the right. An example of Walter Moore's superb photographs can be seen at the bottom of page 33.

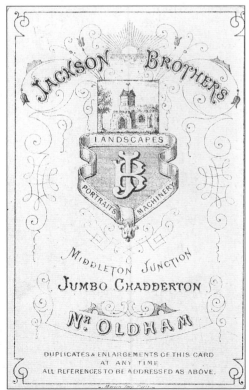

Jackson Brothers were famous photographers in Middleton and Walter Moore worked for them.

Birch Post Office, 1906. It also contained the grocer's shop of A. Leech.

William Yates (bowler hat) with his son-in-law Charles Yates and his cart which operated from his business at 44 Taylor Street.

William Yates's household furnishers at 44 Taylor Street c.1920. Mr and Mrs Yates are in the doorway.

Ratcliffe's shop on Long Street with Miss Yate's sweet shop to the left. Arthur Ratcliffe is standing in his shop doorway with his delivery wagon in front.

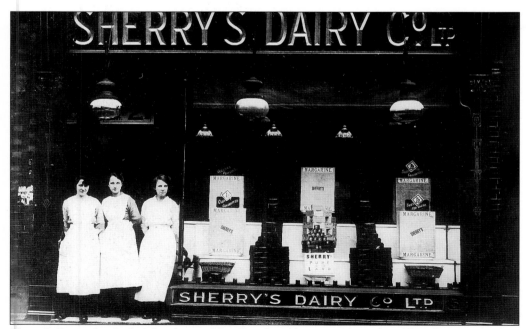

Sherry's Dairy Co. Ltd., Manchester New Road, at the junction with Old Hall Street c.1914. Annie Smithies is on the left.

J. Kent's butcher's shop at 8 Long Street (to the left of the Hare and Hounds Inn). The shop was formerly that of John Lees, clockmaker (see also the photograph of the bottom of page 91).

Miss Jennie Hartley's baby shop, which stood next to the Palace Cinema. Miss Hartley died in 1989 aged 96.

Six
Middleton Mills

The early mills, such as the Middleton Hall Mill and Daniel Burton's Wood Street Mill, were on the River Irk and were water powered. Others, including Hopwood Corn Mill, were on its tributaries. With the advent of steam power and the canal, mills such as the Baytree sprang up alongside the canal at Middleton Junction, taking water from it to cool the engines. Warm spots by the mills were popular with people attempting suicide! The Dane Mills were between the Wince Brook and the railway, making use of the latter to carry coal to the boiler house and transport cotton. Bleach works were at Stakehill and nearby Boarshaw Clough and on the Irk at Rhodes. The prosperity of Middleton was very much linked to the ups and downs of the silk and cotton trades and, in turn, the bleaching mills. The photographs reflect the prosperous times but the cotton famine of the 1860s and the depression of the 1920s and '30s brought deprivation and hardship. The mills also largely dictated the development of housing and many streets were linked to the individual mills whose operatives they housed. Warwick Mill is now a listed building, to be preserved as a reminder of the times when cotton was "king".

Staff of Schwabe's Bleach Works, Rhodes c.1896. Daniel Burton had established the Works around 1784 and sold them to Salis Schwabe in 1832.

Rhodes Reading Room and Library, with Rhodes Works laboratory to the left, 1974. They were on the corner of Manchester Old Road and Broad Street and were built by the Schwabe family.

Schwabe's or Rhodes' Chimney, 5 August 1923. The chimney, added in 1846, was 321 feet high and said to be the tallest brick chimney in Lancashire, if not England. It cost £5,000, with 1.5 million bricks needed to complete it. It was demolished in 1981.

Schwabe's Works was taken over by Calico Printers Limited in 1899. Among prominent visitors was the Gold Coast Chief, Sir Ofori Atta on 13 July 1928. His colourful robes were made from their cloth. C.P.A. closed in 1959.

Schwabe's Works (after it was taken over by Calico Printers Association) and part of the village of Rhodes.

Mrs Dearden who worked at the same four looms at Rhodes Weaving Shed for 25 years. Mr J. Clark is on the left and Mr J. Ronny the right. The Weaving Shed was on Factory Brow, behind Schwabe's Works.

Rhodes Weaving Shed's free trip to Belle Vue, 1911.

Land's End Road Works, Rhodes c.1920. It was owned by Russell (Manchester) Ltd., who were rubber manufacturers. The premises by the Irk were formerly bleach works.

Beamers at Hollows Mill, which was built at Boarshaw about 1874.

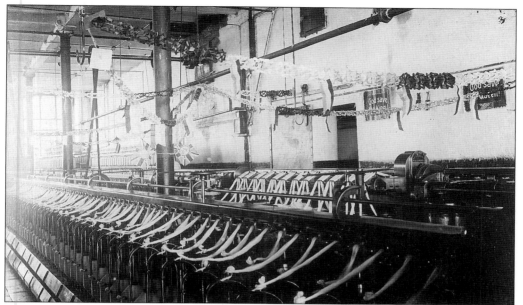

Townley Mill cardroom. The cotton mill, which was off Hanson Street, was opened in 1884 and enlarged in 1910.

Cromer Ring Mill, Boarshaw, opened in 1903. Its closure, as Middleton's last cotton mill in 1978, was a sad loss to the town.

The Dane Mills of Middleton & Tonge Cotton Mill Co. Ltd. in 1879. Railway sidings are to the left with a branch line leading to the boiler house. The Company went bankrupt in 1894.

The Winding and Beaming Room of Neva Mill. Neva was originally comprised of Dane Mills Numbers 1, 2 and 3, John Bunting having taken them over in 1894. He built Times Mill close to them and it became part of the group.

Employees outside Neva Mill (formerly Dane) during the strike of 1912/3.

Birch Mill's steam wagon, 1920. Note the oil lamps. The mill was at the bottom of Langley Lane and provided employment for many of the villagers.

Don Mill, opened in 1899.

Delivering the first bale of cotton to Don Mill Spinning Company Ltd. in 1899.

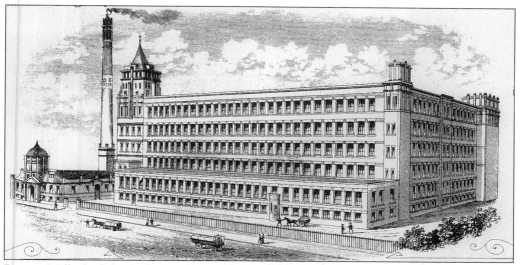

Baytree Mill which backed onto the canal at Middleton Junction. It closed as a cotton mill in 1959.

"The end of the line", demolition of Baytree Mill 1985. The site is now occupied by houses.

Stakehill with the Bleach Works, built by Messrs. Heald Wilson and Co., in the centre. They were later acquired by Samuel Barlow & Sons and finally by Calico Printers Association. During World War II they were used as a detention centre for offenders from the Allied Forces. The Stakehill Industrial Estate now covers this site and much of the surrounding land. It is an important development of modern Middleton, situated close to the M62 motorway and providing employment for many people.

Seven

Best Days Of Our Lives

In the early 1800s, education often started and ended in the Sunday Schools whose chief aim was to teach scholars to read the Bible, Prayer Book and Catechism. From the 1820s the Government gave money to the Church of England to sponsor the "National Society for promoting the education of the Poor in the principles of the Established Church". As a result, National Schools were built across the country including those at Middleton Parish Church, St. Mary, Birch and St. Michael, Tonge. The Non-Conformists likewise received grants. The Education Act of 1870 made education compulsory and the churches were then able to focus more on spiritual teaching in their Sunday Schools. Private schools, such as Hatters, held night school classes in addition to day classes, and before 1870, these were the only source of an education for some people. Ann Aspinall, born in 1817, paid Joseph Kenyon, master of Hatters School, a half pence for each night school attendance and she had to take her own candle! Others, more fortunate, benefitted earlier from the Queen Elizabeth's Grammar School, whose aim was to assist poor scholars in advancing to universities. Thirteen scholars were maintained by endowment each year.

The former Queen Elizabeth's Grammar School (centre), May 1964. It was built in 1572 by Dean Alexander Nowell with Queen Elizabeth presenting the school with an annuity of £20. The original foundation of the school can be traced back to Thomas Langley in 1412, the 1572 building replacing a school that was being housed in the Langley Chapel of St. Leonard's.

The Queen Elizabeth's Grammar School building on Rectory Street. It was demolished in 1995.

Queen Elizabeth's Grammar School Speech Day, 1954-5.

Empire Day celebration at Middleton Parish School c.1920. It was formerly a National School, built in 1842 with Canon Durnford's support.

Birch National School c.1950. It had a stone fireplace surround with the letters of the alphabet on it. It would have seemed natural for village children to gather around it to learn the alphabet, especially on a cold day!

Birch National School group of 1898, with headmaster Mr Smith. There was a single room on each of two floors of the school. The upper was divided by a screen into seniors and juniors and the lower housed the infants. Outside were earth toilets.

Pupils at Tonge National School.

St. Gabriel's School, Middleton Junction c.1912, with teacher Miss Huddart. The desks could be swung around the opposite way to use the top as a back rest. This class was housed in the old church building and the apse can be seen behind the screen.

Hatters School House, Stott Lane, 13 April 1943. It bore the inscription "School House. Rent free 1754". Squire Hopwood paid the fees of children of workers on his Hopwood Estate and children from Hebers' Workhouse also attended the school.

John Howorth's School, Boardman Lane, Rhodes Green. The inscription read "John and Hannah Howorth 1782 the School". According to directories of the time it was also called the Dungeon School. It was demolished in 1975.

Rhodes School group of 1920, with Frank Cosgrove second from the left on the second row. This Walker Street School was built in 1884 by Salis Schwabe's family and was also known as Schwabe's School. The Schwabe family gave it to Middleton Corporation Finance Committee in 1903.

Rhodes School Walk, 1928. The back of the photograph is marked "Co-op Walk" but it looks like an Empire Day celebration.

Boarshaw Primary School Harvest Festival, 1937.

Boarshaw School decorated for the Coronation of 1937, with Headmaster Albert Hartley at the back left.

Eight
Fun and Festivals

Just as the church was a major provider of early education, it was also the instigator of some of the festivals, wakes and rushbearing being two of them. Wakes is a name of Saxon origin meaning a waking or watching. People would sit up all night in the church on the eve of the dedication festival. Rushbearing was the ancient custom, prevalent in Lancashire, of gathering rushes and strewing them on the earth floor of the churches, providing a covering. When floors became flagged the covering was not as necessary, but as with the wakes the custom continued long after the association with the church ceased. Middleton's last rush cart was made in 1883, but the annual holiday at the wakes and rushbearing (both being at the same time) continued, on the penultimate Saturday in August in Middleton. The mills closed and it became a popular time for weddings. On Wakes Saturday 1936, Billy Wellens organised cars for 21 weddings, the firm managing to do 18 of them themselves, with the first at 8 a.m. and the last at 6 p.m. It was quite common in Rochdale to be married at 8 a.m. and to be in Blackpool by 10 a.m. Maybe it took a little longer from Middleton!

Something that draws me to Middleton!

THERE IS SOMETING THAT DRAWS ME TO MIDDLETON

Middleton Rushbearing, celebrated on the penultimate Saturday in August. This rush cart of 1883 was the last to be built in Middleton. Robert Standring is the leader in the centre.

Middleton Wakes. Villages such as Birch would also have stalls lining the streets at the Wakes.

A rushbearing wedding. Herbert and Alice Cosgrove were married at All Saints, Rhodes, 24 August 1912.

An Alkrington Hall wedding, 14 July 1923. Amy Sadie Colson, daughter of Mr and Mrs George F. Colson, (owners of the Hall) married Robert Harris Etchells.

Mock weddings, sometimes called Village or Rainbow Weddings, were a popular feature in Heywood Carnivals, where the Rhodes entry was often the winner. The above is the Rhodes Victory Wedding of 1918 with Mr Ogden as the right hand driver.

Celebrating the Diamond Jubilee of the reign of Queen Victoria, 22 June 1897. The umbrellas are for protection from the sun not rain! The programme for the day included processions, illuminations, concerts, pageants, the firing of salutes and other celebrations. The Public Library and Jubilee Park on Long Street became lasting reminders of the celebration.

Illuminations in Central Gardens, marking the Silver Jubilee of George V, 1935.

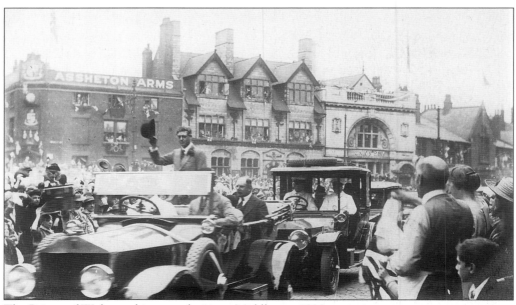

The Prince of Wales on his second visit to Middleton, 1923.

The Peace Parade at the end of World War I, Manchester Old Road.

The Bonfire at Tandle Hill celebrating the end of World War I. Tandle Hill can be seen for miles around and its name is thought to be derived from the Celtic word "tan", meaning fire. Its main approach was originally from the Haggate side, the word Haggate being translated as "road to heathen temple".

"Mary, Mary, quite contrary". A decorated tableau at Boothroyden in the Peace Procession. Behind are cottages at the bottom of Boardman Lane, which have since been demolished.

The May Pole and May Queen festival outside the Old Grammar School c.1922. Local historian Margaret Smith is the tall girl to the left of centre and her sister Jean (now McMullen) is on the extreme left.

Outside the Barber's Arms Inn, Manchester Old Road, Rhodes.

Rhodes Cricket Team, Broad Street c.1928 (see also the photograph at the bottom of page 26).

Middleton Borough Band outside Tonge Cricket Club, 1923.

Tonge Church Brass Band passing Middleton Station entrance (Oldham Road), 1926.

The Band Stand, Jubilee Park.

Hounds at the bottom of New Lane, with Mellalieu Street behind, c.1904. The bearded policeman in the centre is P.C. MacDonald but the identity of the hounds pack is not so certain! The Marland or Foxdenton Hounds are the most popular guesses.

North Manchester Golf Club's former H.Q. at the corner of Blackley New Road and Middleton Road, with Bowker Vale Station to the left. The club moved to their present location in Manchester Old Road in 1925.

Dedicating the Verjuice Stone (used to extract juice from apples) at St. Leonard's Church, 9 September 1990. The stone was discovered during excavations at Langley Hall. Carl Goldberg and Stanley White are second and third from left.